THE
WHITE LOTUS

OFFICIAL
COCKTAIL COLLECTION

THE
WHITE LOTUS

OFFICIAL
COCKTAIL COLLECTION

INSIGHT
EDITIONS

SAN RAFAEL · LOS ANGELES · LONDON

CONTENTS

IT'S COCKTAIL HOUR

Welcome to the world of The White Lotus—the warm, sun-washed resort paradise that offers an exclusive, opulent experience for only the most special guests. And you're here! You're finally here. The sand is warm, the waves are turquoise, the towels are fresh and soft. Your friends are here, too, and they are beautiful. Would you like a drink? An Aperol spritz? A sunset sangria? A tall, vodka soda, rimmed with a chunk of lime, perfect for toasting? Take a sip. It's time to relax.

Whether you're on a luxury yacht in the Sicilian waters, on a beach in blossom-scented Thailand, or enjoying a candlelit dinner with the Hawaiian breezes blowing over your table, you're probably going to want a cocktail to get you in the mood. Tropical flavors, floral infusions, and fruity, icy concoctions offer a taste of resort paradise. Add mango, papaya, and lychee to bubbles or steep spicy Thai chiles in tequila or fragrant white tea in vodka, then take your drink down to the beach. It's almost time for the sunset. There's a lounge chair waiting for you on the sand. Get comfortable, admire the light on the water, and listen to the ice clinking in your glass. You made it. You've arrived. Now enjoy your drink.

WITHIN THESE PAGES

If you're trapped in your scrubby suburban backyard or claustrophobic apartment balcony, don't despair—you'll find proverbial warm resort breezes within these pages. Invite a few friends over and use these recipes as The White Lotus–inspired party guide you've been looking for.

The six sections inside cover all manner of resort libations:

TROPICAL ELIXIRS are the tranquility of the tropics in a glass. Let the stress melt away with every sip.

SUNSET SIPS is a set of drinks for the magic hour, that time when the sun is low and golden, and the day is done. These pours are your liquid relaxation.

POOLSIDE PLEASURES is the cocktail equivalent of a dive into crystal-clear water. Tall and thirst-quenching, these vibrant mixtures are just what you need after that swim. Or before the swim. Or *instead* of the swim.

ISLAND INFUSIONS are there when you're ready to explore a bit and are our take on some local specialties. After all, why travel far from home if you're going to play it safe?

BOTANICAL BLISS showcases the plants and flowers that surround any beautiful White Lotus vacation. Select a recipe from the section and you'll find herbal and floral infusions that are perfect resort sips.

MOCKTAIL ESCAPES are here when your head needs just a bit of a break. You won't sacrifice any interest or flavor, but your liver might send up a tiny "thank you" in return.

SHAKE, STIR, MIX & SERVE

Gorgeous drinks deserve gorgeous barware. There's no need to stock up on every bar tool ever made, but an investment in a few basics will make mixing the drinks almost as delightful as quaffing them.

THE MUDDLER: This slender tool with a blunt end crushes herbs, like mint or basil, or fruit at the bottom of a cocktail shaker or glass to release flavors and oils before adding the liquid ingredients.

THE BARSPOON: A barspoon has a twisted handle and is long and slim for efficient stirring.

THE DUAL JIGGER: This small measuring tool has one small cup on one end and one large cup on the other. The small cup holds 1 ounce, and the large cup holds 1 1/2 ounces.

THE SHAKER: There are two types of shakers: a Boston shaker, a two-piece version with a small cup fit into a larger cup for easy shaking; and a cobbler shaker, a three-piece shaker with one cup, a lid, and a strainer. Choose the type that you like the best.

THE STRAINER: A sieve that fits inside your cocktail shaker that keeps ice or other solid chunks from falling into your drink as you pour. Double straining a cocktail means using both a regular cocktail strainer and a fine-mesh strainer to pour the drink into the glass. This technique helps remove smaller ice shards, fruit pulp, herbs, and other fine particles, resulting in a smoother and clearer cocktail.

THE MIXING GLASS: A mixing glass is a specialized, heavy glass used by bartenders to stir and mix cocktails.

GLASSWARE: Drinks work well in different shapes of glasses. Highball glasses, rocks, martini, coupes, hurricanes, margarita, wineglasses, Champagne flutes, goblet, and copper mugs will complete any collection.

A TOUCH OF SWEETNESS

Channel the effortless glamour of The White Lotus with flavored syrups, crafted in-house or purchased, to add nuanced flavors without overpowering the spirit you are using. From dragon fruit to mango, to lychee, these sweet additions bring a touch of paradise to every drink, elevating your cocktail creations with every sip.

Honey Syrup

MAKES 1 CUP

½ cup honey
½ cup water

In a small saucepan, combine the honey and water. Place the saucepan over medium heat and cook, stirring constantly, until the honey is completely dissolved. Once the mixture comes to a gentle simmer, reduce the heat to low and let it simmer for 2 minutes, stirring occasionally. Remove the saucepan from the heat and let cool to room temperature. Once cooled, transfer to a clean bottle or jar with a tight-fitting lid. Store the honey syrup in the refrigerator for up to 2 weeks.

Simple Syrup

MAKES 1 CUP

1 cup water
1 cup sugar

In a small saucepan, combine the water and sugar. Place the saucepan over medium heat and bring to a gentle simmer. Continue to simmer, stirring occasionally, until all the sugar is dissolved, 5-10 minutes. Remove from the heat. Let cool to room temperature. Once cooled, transfer to a clean bottle or jar with a tight-fitting lid. Store the simple syrup in the refrigerator for up to 1 month.

Butterfly Pea Tea Syrup

MAKES 1½ CUPS

1 cup water

2 tablespoons dried butterfly pea flowers or 2 butterfly pea tea bags

1 cup sugar

In a small saucepan, bring the water to a boil. Once boiling, remove from the heat and add the pea flowers or tea bags. Let steep for 5-10 minutes, depending on the desired color intensity. If using loose flowers, strain through a fine-mesh sieve or cheesecloth to remove any sediment. Return the strained tea to the saucepan over medium heat and bring to a gentle simmer. Add the sugar and continue to simmer, stirring occasionally, until all the sugar is dissolved, 5-10 minutes. Remove from the heat and let cool to room temperature. Transfer to a clean bottle or jar with a tight-fitting lid and store in the refrigerator for up to 2 weeks.

Dragon Fruit Syrup

MAKES 1½ CUPS

1 cup water

1 cup sugar

1 cup cubed fresh or frozen dragon fruit

In a saucepan, combine the water, sugar, and dragon fruit and place over medium heat until the sugar dissolves, then simmer for 3 minutes. Remove from the heat and let cool to room temperature. Strain through a fine-mesh sieve or cheesecloth into a clean bottle or jar with a tight-fitting lid. Refrigerate for 2-3 weeks.

Passion Fruit Syrup

MAKES 1½ CUPS

1 cup water

1 cup sugar

1 cup passion fruit pulp

In a medium saucepan, combine sugar and water. Bring to a simmer over medium heat, stirring until sugar dissolves completely. Remove from the heat and let cool to room temperature. Strain through a fine-mesh sieve or cheesecloth into a clean bottle or jar with a tight-fitting lid. Refrigerate for 2-3 weeks.

Lemongrass Syrup

MAKES 1½ CUPS

2 stalks lemongrass

1 cup water

1 cup sugar

Trim the root end and tough outer layers from the lemongrass stalks. Cut the stalks into smaller pieces and lightly crush them with a knife or mallet to release the oils.

Combine the water, sugar, and crushed lemongrass in a saucepan over medium heat. Cook, stirring, until the sugar dissolves. Simmer for 10–15 minutes on low heat. Strain the hot syrup in a fine-mesh sieve to remove the lemongrass. Cool to room temperature and store in a clean bottle or jar with a tight-fitting lid in the refrigerator for up to 2 weeks.

Lychee Syrup

MAKES 1½ CUPS

1 cup water

1 cup sugar

1 cup fresh peeled and pitted or canned lychees

In a small saucepan, combine the water and sugar. Place the saucepan over medium heat and bring to a gentle simmer. Add the lychees and simmer, stirring occasionally, until the sugar is dissolved, about 10 minutes. Remove from the heat and let cool to room temperature. Once cooled, strain the lychee syrup through a fine-mesh sieve or cheesecloth to remove the solids. Transfer into a clean bottle or jar with a tight-fitting lid. Store in the refrigerator for up to 2 weeks.

Ginger Syrup

MAKES 1½ CUPS

1 cup water

1 cup sugar

½ cup peeled fresh ginger slices

In a small saucepan, combine the water and sugar. Place the saucepan over medium heat and bring to a gentle simmer. Add the sliced ginger and simmer for 15–20 minutes. Remove from the heat and let steep for 10 minutes. Strain through a fine-mesh sieve to remove the solids into a clean bottle or jar with a tight-fitting lid. Store in the refrigerator for up to 2 weeks.

Mango Syrup

MAKES 1½ CUPS

1 cup water

1 cup sugar

1 cup cubed fresh or frozen mango

In a small saucepan, combine the water and sugar. Place the saucepan over medium heat and bring to a gentle simmer. Add the cubed mango, reduce the heat to low, and simmer, stirring occasionally, until the sugar is dissolved, about 10 minutes. Remove from the heat and let cool to room temperature. Once cooled, strain the mango syrup through a fine-mesh sieve or cheesecloth into a clean bowl, pressing down on the mango pieces to extract as much liquid as possible. Transfer the strained mango syrup to a clean bottle or jar with a tight-fitting lid. Store in the refrigerator for up to 2 weeks.

Jasmine Syrup

MAKES 1½ CUPS

1 cup water

1 cup sugar

1 tablespoon dried food-grade jasmine flowers or 2 jasmine tea bags

In a small saucepan, combine the water, sugar, and dried jasmine flowers or tea bags. Place the saucepan over medium heat and bring to a gentle simmer. Reduce the heat to low and simmer for 10 minutes, stirring occasionally, until the sugar is completely dissolved. Remove from the heat and let cool to room temperature. Once cooled, strain through a fine-mesh sieve or cheesecloth to remove the solids into a clean bottle or jar with a tight-fitting lid. Store in the refrigerator for up to 2 weeks.

Thai Chile Syrup

MAKES 1½ CUPS

1 cup water

1 cup sugar

4-6 red Thai chiles, sliced (adjust the quantity based on desired spiciness)

In a small saucepan, combine the water, sugar, and chiles. Place the saucepan over medium heat and bring to a gentle simmer. Reduce the heat to low and simmer for 10 minutes, stirring occasionally, until the sugar is completely dissolved. Remove from the heat and let cool to room temperature. Once cooled, strain through a fine-mesh sieve or cheesecloth to remove the chile pieces into a clean bottle or jar with a tight-fitting lid. Store in the refrigerator for up to 2 weeks.

Matcha Syrup

MAKES 1½ CUPS

1 cup water

1 cup sugar

2 tablespoons high-quality matcha powder

In a small saucepan, combine the water and sugar. Place the saucepan over medium heat and stir until the sugar is completely dissolved. Once the mixture comes to a gentle simmer, reduce the heat to low. Sift the matcha powder through a fine-mesh sieve or cheesecloth into the saucepan to remove any clumps. Whisk the matcha powder into the sugar and water mixture until it's completely dissolved. Simmer the mixture for about 5 minutes, stirring occasionally. Remove from the heat and let cool to room temperature. Once cooled, transfer the matcha syrup to a clean bottle or jar with a tight-fitting lid. Store in the refrigerator for up to 2 weeks.

INFUSED SPIRITS

Elevate your cocktail creations with a touch of luxury. Explore the art of infusing spirits with exotic flavors, from delicate white tea vodka to fiery Thai chile tequila. Tailor your drinks to your personal oasis, just like the discerning guests of The White Lotus.

White Tea-Infused Vodka

MAKES 1 CUP

8 ounces vodka

2-3 tablespoons loose-leaf white tea

Pour the vodka into a clean glass jar or bottle with a tight-fitting lid. Add the white tea. Make sure the tea is completely submerged in the vodka. Seal the jar or bottle tightly and give it a good shake to mix the ingredients. Place the jar or bottle in a cool, dark place for at least 24 hours or up to 48 hours if you like a stronger tea flavor, shaking it occasionally to agitate the mixture. Strain the vodka into a bowl through a fine-mesh sieve or cheesecloth to remove the tea leaves. Transfer the infused vodka to a clean jar or bottle with a tight-fitting lid. Store in the refrigerator or a cool, dark place until ready to use, up to 2 months.

Butterfly Pea Flower–Infused Vodka

MAKES 1 CUP

½ cup dried butterfly pea flowers

8 ounces vodka

Place the dried butterfly pea flowers in a clean jar or bottle. Pour the vodka over the flowers until they are fully submerged. Seal the jar or bottle and let it infuse at room temperature for at least 24 hours or up to 48 hours for a stronger flavor. Once infused, strain through a fine-mesh sieve or cheesecloth into a bowl to remove the pea flowers. Transfer the infused vodka to a clean jar or bottle with a tight-fitting lid. Store in a cool dark place until ready to use, up to 2 months.

Pineapple-Infused Tequila

MAKES 3 CUPS

1 ripe pineapple

1 bottle (750 ml) blanco tequila

Peel the pineapple and cut it into small chunks or slices. Place the pineapple pieces into a clean, wide-mouthed glass jar or bottle. Pour the tequila over the pineapple; it should completely cover the fruit. Seal the jar or bottle tightly and give it a gentle shake to mix the ingredients. Store the jar or bottle in a cool, dark place for at least 3 days to allow the flavors to infuse. You can leave it longer for a stronger pineapple flavor. After infusing, strain the tequila into a bowl through a fine-mesh sieve or cheesecloth to remove the pineapple pieces. Transfer the infused tequila back into its original bottle or a clean container for storage. The infused tequila will keep for up to 2 months stored in a cool dark place.

Strawberry-Infused Campari

MAKES 1 CUP

½ cup sliced ripe strawberries

8 ounces Campari

Place the sliced strawberries in a clean jar or bottle. Pour the Campari over the strawberries, making sure they are fully submerged. Seal the jar or bottle and let it infuse at room temperature for at least 24 hours or up to 48 hours if you like a stronger strawberry flavor. Once infused, strain through a fine-mesh sieve or cheesecloth into a bowl to remove the strawberries. Transfer the infused Campari to a clean jar or bottle with a tight-fitting lid. Store in a cool dark place for up to 2 months.

Thai Chile-Infused Tequila

MAKES 1 CUP

2-3 red Thai chiles

8 ounces blanco tequila

Slice the Thai chiles lengthwise to expose the seeds and membranes and place them in a clean glass jar or bottle with a tight-fitting lid. Pour in the tequila ensuring that the chiles are fully submerged. Seal the jar or bottle tightly and shake gently to mix the ingredients. Place the jar or bottle in a cool, dark place to infuse for at least 24 hours. After 24 hours, taste the infused tequila to check the level of spiciness. If you'd like it spicier, you can let it infuse for up to 24 more hours. Strain the infused tequila into a bowl through a fine-mesh sieve or cheesecloth to remove the chiles. Transfer the infused tequila to a clean jar or bottle with a tight-fitting lid. Store in the refrigerator or a cool, dark place until ready to use, up to 2 months.

TROPICAL ELIXIRS

Exotic Flavors

A journey to The White Lotus has many destinations but each one is a tropical paradise made just for you. Hawaiian blossoms might drip over your head as you accept a glass clinking with ice, or perhaps ferns crowd your feet when you make your way to the bar over a bamboo path. Either way, you'll know you've found serenity, beauty, luxury, and relaxation. A special cocktail in hand is the perfect companion to take with you on this journey—let's set off together.

THE WHITE LOTUS ARRIVAL COCKTAIL

It's been a long journey. You're a bit sticky, perhaps a bit thirsty. But paradise is almost here. Just step into the courtyard and reach for a glass of this vodka-based cocktail—we've kept it simple with pineapple juice and a squeeze of lemon, but we've made it special with a white-tea infused vodka. Admire your glass beaded with moisture, then take a long sip—paradise has arrived.

1½ ounces White Tea-Infused Vodka (page 19)

2 ounces pineapple juice

½ ounce fresh lemon juice

½ ounce Honey Syrup (page 12)

Fresh mint sprigs, for garnish

Add the vodka, pineapple juice, lemon juice, and Honey Syrup to a cocktail shaker. Add ice and shake for 30 seconds until chilled. Strain into a rocks glass with fresh ice. Garnish with fresh mint sprigs.

PINEAPPLE SUNSET MIMOSA

It's never too early for a cocktail at The White Lotus, especially one so elegantly served in a Champagne flute. Give the mimosa a Hawaiian twist with pineapple juice instead of orange and drop in grenadine for a beautiful red-to-orange blush. Fill your flute and enjoy the bubbles along with the view.

3 ounces chilled
pineapple juice

3 ounces chilled
Champagne or sparkling
wine (brut or extra dry)

½ ounce grenadine

Pineapple slice, for garnish

Pour the pineapple juice into to a Champagne flute. Add the Champagne. Slowly pour in the grenadine and allow it to sink to the bottom of the glass. Garnish with the pineapple slice.

HAWAIIAN HONEYMOON

Reposado tequila is an excellent mixing liquor. It's strong enough to stand up to the bite of pineapple and ginger, which makes it the perfect The White Lotus sipper. Any honeymooner coming to the resort might need a bit of liquid courage, especially when faced with your brand-new spouse across the lunch table after a night of . . . well, sometimes it's better not to say. Pour one of these to ease any tension—one for you and one for them.

2 ounces reposado tequila

1½ ounces purchased pineapple ginger juice

½ ounce Honey Syrup (page 12)

Pineapple wedge, for garnish

Orchid blossoms, for garnish (optional)

Add the tequila, pineapple ginger juice, and Honey Syrup to a cocktail shaker. Add ice and shake for 30 seconds until chilled. Strain into a hurricane glass. Garnish with pineapple wedge and orchid blossom (if using).

THE PINEAPPLE SUITE

What could be more delicious than a rum punch on a sun-bright day? In our version of this classic cocktail, grenadine is replaced with a homemade honey syrup, and we keep it simple with light rum and fresh lime juice. Add palm trees, shake on a dusting of white sand, and take an icy sip. You're officially on vacation.

2 ounces light rum

1 ounce pineapple juice

½ ounce fresh lime juice

½ ounce Honey Syrup (page 12)

Pineapple wedge, for garnish

Pineapple fronds, for garnish (optional)

Add the rum, pineapple juice, lime juice, and Honey Syrup to a cocktail shaker. Add ice and shake for 30 seconds to chill. Strain into a rocks glass over fresh ice. Garnish with a pineapple wedge and pineapple fronds (if using).

HIDDEN ROMANCE

*Shadowy nooks and shrouded corners are even better with a
glass of our blushing-pink cocktail. The delicate sweetness of
dragon fruit syrup gets a bump from the smoky bite of mezcal.
Shake up one of these icy concoctions and sip it with your own
secret lover—even if it's just for a night.*

2 ounces mezcal

½ ounce dry vermouth

¾ ounce Dragon Fruit
Syrup (page 14)

Dragon fruit slice or
dehydrated lime slice,
for garnish

Add the mezcal, dry vermouth, and Dragon Fruit Syrup to a
cocktail shaker. Add ice and shake for 30 seconds until chilled.
Strain into a chilled martini or coupe glass. Garnish with a slice of
dragon fruit or a dehydrated lime.

PARADISE MARGARITA

Fruit makes a bright showing here with this take on the ultimate vacation cocktail—the margarita. Mango and passion fruit complement a tequila imbued with pineapple, while Cointreau and lime do their bit for tradition. After a good shake, strain into a sugar-rimmed glass. Good choice, you.

1½ ounces Pineapple-Infused Tequila (page 20)

½ ounce Cointreau

½ ounce mango juice

1 ounce fresh lime juice

½ ounce Passion Fruit Syrup (page 14; if passion fruit is hard to find, use purchased syrup)

Pineapple wedge or lime wheel, for garnish

Fresh mint sprig, for garnish

Prepare your sugar-rimmed glass. Rub a lime wedge around the rim of the margarita glass to moisten it evenly with lime juice. Then, pour granulated sugar onto a small plate and gently dip the moistened rim into the sugar, ensuring it adheres evenly. Add the tequila, Cointreau, mango juice, lime juice, and Passion Fruit Syrup to a cocktail shaker. Add ice and shake for 30 seconds until chilled. Strain into the prepared glass with fresh ice. Garnish with a pineapple wedge or lime wheel and fresh mint sprig.

STORMY HAWAIIAN

On a crystal-blue tropical day without a cloud in the sky, enjoy our fruity take on the island standby, the dark and stormy. We've added a splash of pineapple juice to spicy ginger beer and rich dark rum. Ask for it at the swim-up bar—there's no need to even get out of the pool to enjoy it.

2 ounces dark rum

1 ounce pineapple juice

½ ounce fresh lime juice

4 ounces ginger beer

Lime, for garnish

Fill a highball glass with ice. Add the dark rum, pineapple juice, and lime juice. Top with ginger beer and stir to combine. Garnish with a lime wedge.

THAI GUAVA BLISS

*A tropical cocktail with a hint of the Sicilian shores, this
unusual marriage of Aperol and guava is actually a perfect
pairing. The guava, with a flavor often described as a mixture of
pear and strawberry, tempers the bitterness of the liqueur, with
a bit of welcome burn from tequila. Sip, sip, and sip—and then
order up another one from your favorite bartender.*

2 ounces blanco tequila

1 ounce guava puree

¾ ounce Aperol liqueur

½ ounce fresh lime juice

Lime wheel, for garnish

Add the tequila, guava puree, Aperol, and lime juice to a cocktail
shaker. Add ice and shake for 30 seconds until chilled. Strain into
a rocks glass over fresh ice. Garnish with a lime wheel.

MANGO THAI-TINI

A martini has just three ingredients: vodka or gin, vermouth, and a dash of bitters. But in the tropics, we like excess. We've tossed the vermouth and the bitters and instead added mango, coconut, and lime for a cocktail more suited to a bikini than a blazer. You can take this one shaken—because the rules are a little different in the tropics.

1½ ounces vodka

1 ounce mango juice

1 ounce coconut water

½ ounce fresh lime juice

½ ounce Simple Syrup (page 12)

Mango slices, for garnish

Add the vodka, mango juice, coconut water, lime juice, and Simple Syrup to a cocktail shaker. Add ice and shake for 30 seconds until chilled. Strain into a rocks glass over fresh ice or into a chilled martini glass. Garnish with a couple of slices of fresh mango.

THE PALM SUITE

Welcome to the Palm Suite! Take a look at the plunge pool. Beautiful, isn't it? And the view! Sapphire skies to match the sapphire water. Now it's time for a drink. Where's the bar? Ah, there it is and the makings for the eponymous cocktail are right in front of you. Our twist on a Paloma replaces grapefruit with passion fruit liqueur, so you can start enjoying the tropics as soon as you set down your bags.

1½ ounces blanco tequila

½ ounce passion fruit liqueur

1 ounce fresh lime juice

½ ounce agave syrup

Passion fruit half or lime wedge, for garnish

Orchid blossom, for garnish (optional)

Add the tequila, passion fruit liqueur, lime juice, and agave syrup to a cocktail shaker. Add ice and shake for 30 seconds until chilled. Strain into a rocks glass over fresh ice. Garnish with a passion fruit half or lime wedge and orchid blossom (if using).

SUNSET SIPS

Cocktails for Relaxation

Sunset is the most beautiful time of any day—but sunset over the ocean is a special experience, whether you're watching from a restaurant patio or a lounge chair on the beach. Perhaps you're watching through the windows of an opulent lounge while the piano plays and a bartender awaits your order. In that case, pull up your barstool because we've assembled a collection of sips that are perfect for the twilight hours when anything—*anything*—might happen.

THE WHITE LOTUS LOUNGE OLD-FASHIONED

When the piano music floats through the air and the bartender starts shaking up his concoctions, you can glide up to the bar and order up one of our special lounge-tails—or even mix it up in your own kitchen if the bartender's off for the night. We've given this drink a special twist with Italian Galliano liqueur, along with the bitters, sugar, and whiskey that make up any decent old-fashioned.

1 sugar cube

2–3 dashes Angostura bitters

2 ounces bourbon or
rye whiskey

½ ounce Galliano liqueur

Orange twist, for garnish

Cocktail cherries, for
garnish

Put the sugar cube into a rocks glass. Add 2–3 dashes of bitters directly onto the sugar cube. Muddle the sugar cube with the bitters until it's well mixed and slightly dissolved. Add a few ice cubes to the glass. Pour in the whiskey and Galliano. Stir gently with a bar spoon to combine the ingredients. Grab the ends of the orange twist between your fingers, place it over the glass, and give it a gentle twist to express the oils into the glass, then drop it in. Garnish with the cherries.

I JUST LOVE YOU

*Bittersweet, biting, and unexpected. Is it the mysteries of love—
or the cocktail in your hand? Here, the mysterious herbal blend
that makes up amaro liqueur gets a bump of fizz from prosecco
and soda water. Perhaps your own love life needs a few bubbles?
Mix up this spritzer for yourself and . . . whomever you want.*

1½ ounces amaro

3 ounces prosecco

1 ounce soda water

Lime wheel, for garnish

Fill a wineglass with ice. Pour the amaro, prosecco, and soda water into the glass. Stir gently with a bar spoon to combine. Garnish with a lime wheel.

LET'S FUN! NEGRONI

A negroni is the ultimate Italian cocktail, best poured over a large ice cube. Here, make your own fun by infusing Campari with fresh strawberries then allowing them to steep for a couple of days. You'll capture the summery fragrance of the berry. This drink is perfect for sipping at sunset by the pool, on the beach, or on your porch—choose your own form of vacation paradise.

1 ounce Strawberry-Infused Campari (page 20)

1 ounce gin

1 ounce sweet vermouth

Fresh strawberry slices, for garnish (optional)

Pour the Strawberry-Infused Campari, gin, and sweet vermouth into a mixing glass. Add ice and stir with a bar spoon for about 30 seconds to chill and properly dilute the drink. Strain the mixture into a chilled rocks glass over a large ice cube. Garnish with fresh strawberry slices (if using).

FULL MOON MARGARITA

Butterfly pea flower tea turns any cocktail a beautiful violet color—perfect for a special margarita like this one. When you add this tea syrup to tequila and cream of coconut, you'll create a gorgeous concoction that you can strain over ice. Take it outside and enjoy the moon's beauty, whether it floats over the Sicilian waves or your own backyard stoop.

2 ounces blanco tequila

1 ounce fresh lime juice

½ ounce cream of coconut

½ ounce Butterfly Pea Tea Syrup (page 14)

Lime wheel or butterfly pea flowers, for garnish

Add the tequila, lime juice, cream of coconut, and Butterfly Pea Tea Syrup to a cocktail shaker. Add ice and shake for 30 seconds until chilled. Strain into a rocks glass over fresh ice. Garnish with a lime wheel or butterfly pea flowers.

REJUVENATING BOURBON SOUR

Long, bright days on the white sand, swims in the warm turquoise water, wandering walks down paths dripping with tropical greenery—look, resort living is a hard life. Sometimes, you need a little rejuvenation. The proverbial face-slap of lemon and ginger in this sour-style cocktail will perk you up during the sleepy twilight hours. Have another, then get ready for the night ahead.

2 ounces bourbon

¾ ounce fresh
lemon juice

½ ounce Ginger Syrup
(page 15)

1 egg white*

Lemon ribbon, for garnish

Add the bourbon, lemon juice, Ginger Syrup, and egg white to a cocktail shaker. Shake vigorously without ice for 30 seconds. Add ice and shake again for 30 seconds until chilled. Double strain into a chilled rocks glass. Garnish with a lemon ribbon.

*If you have food safety concerns, you may wish to avoid drinks with raw egg whites.

WHITE LINEN IN THAILAND

The delicious white linen cocktail usually features gin, lemon juice, and elderflower liqueur. We've added a spicy twist by replacing the elderflower with Thai chile syrup. Lime takes the place of lemon, and this newly spicy sipper is cooled with cucumber slices. Shake and strain into an icy glass and enjoy in the flickering twilight.

3 cucumber slices

2 ounces gin

1 ounce fresh lime juice

½ ounce Thai Chile Syrup (page 17)

1 ounce soda water

Cucumber ribbon or red Thai chile, for garnish

Put the cucumber slices in a cocktail shaker and gently muddle them. Add the gin, lime juice, and Thai Chile Syrup. Add ice and shake for 30 seconds until chilled. Strain into a rocks glass over fresh ice. Top with the soda water. Garnish with a cucumber ribbon or a red Thai chile—or both.

NIGHT IN NOTO

As the hot, bright day draws to a close, mix up a reverse take on the tequila sunrise—here, a tequila sunset that pays homage to that dreamy moment when velvety dusk drapes the landscape and the cool night air floats in on the waves. The bite of Aperol and grapefruit is softened by the sweetness of simple syrup, making a cocktail perfect for floating in the lighted pool, walking on the nighttime beach, or just lying on the couch.

1½ ounces blanco tequila

1 ounce fresh
grapefruit juice

½ ounce Aperol liqueur

½ ounce Simple Syrup
(page 12)

Grapefruit slice,
for garnish

Hibiscus petals,
for garnish (optional)

Add the tequila, grapefruit juice, Aperol, and Simple Syrup to a cocktail shaker. Add ice and shake for 30 seconds until chilled. Strain into a rocks glass over fresh ice. Garnish with a grapefruit slice and hibiscus petals (if using).

GIN-LIGHTENED COOLER

Coolers are the perfect late-afternoon quaffs, especially if you find yourself poolside on a steamy afternoon. These icy mixtures of fruit juices, clear spirits, and fun flavors are ripe for creativity. We've made this gin cooler special with the addition of homemade lemongrass syrup—keep it in the fridge for up to 2 weeks and splash some into your beverage whenever you need a little gin-lightenment.

2 ounces gin

1 ounce pressed coconut water

½ ounce fresh lime juice

½ ounce Lemongrass Syrup (page 15)

Lime wheel, for garnish

Add the gin, coconut water, lime juice, and Lemongrass Syrup to a cocktail shaker. Add ice and shake for 30 seconds until chilled. Strain into a rocks glass over fresh ice. Garnish with a lime wheel.

GREEN GARDEN SOUR

The Japanese rice-based spirit, sake, has a clean, slightly sweet taste that pairs beautifully with spicy ginger and earthy, bitter matcha. Mixing in a whipped egg white marries these Asian-inspired flavors with a sour-style cocktail creating a special resort-level libation. Close your eyes and picture a garden dripping with tropical flowers as you sip.

1½ ounces dry sake

½ ounce ginger liqueur

½ ounce Matcha Syrup (page 17)

½ ounce fresh lemon juice

1 egg white*

Add the sake, ginger liqueur, Matcha Syrup, lemon juice, and egg white to a cocktail shaker. Shake vigorously without ice for 30 seconds. Add ice and shake again for 30 seconds until chilled. Double strain into a chilled coupe glass.

*If you have food safety concerns, you may wish to avoid drinks with raw egg whites.

OREO® COOKIE CAKE MARTINI

Sometimes, you need a little decadence. Sometimes you need a lot of decadence—and a little dollop of whipped cream. Here's a chocolate cookie cake in quaffable form, with two kinds of sweet liqueur (yes, please), shaken with vodka, and of course, crushed cookies—because why wouldn't you? Try this martini instead of dessert—or along with it.

Chocolate syrup, for rimming the glass

Crushed Oreo cookies, for rimming the glass

2 ounces vodka

1 ounce Irish cream liqueur

1 ounce chocolate liqueur

Whipped cream, for garnish (optional)

Pour some chocolate syrup onto a small plate. Put the crushed Oreo cookies on a second small plate. Dip the rim of a martini glass into the syrup, then into the crushed Oreo cookies to create a chocolate and cookie rim. Add the vodka, Irish cream, and chocolate liqueur to a cocktail shaker. Add ice and shake for 10–15 seconds until well chilled. Strain into the prepared glass. If desired, top with a dollop of whipped cream.

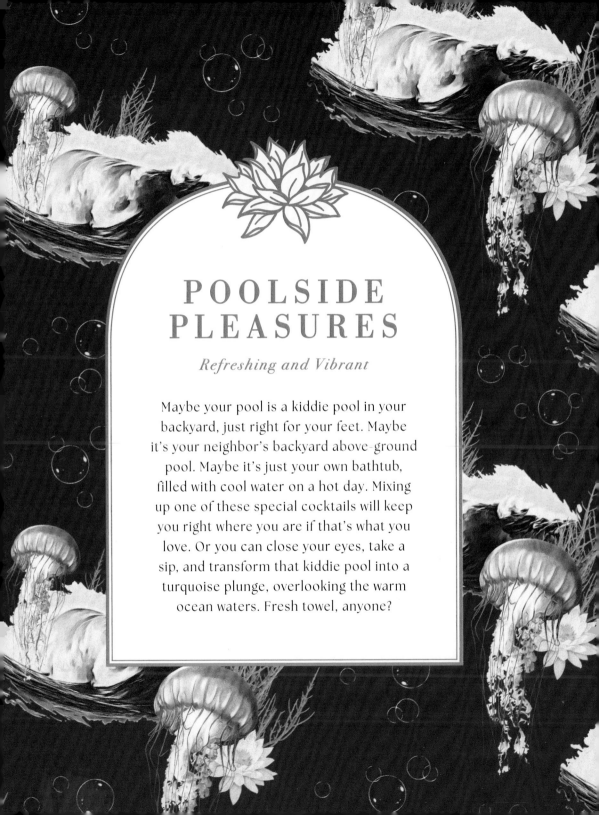

POOLSIDE PLEASURES

Refreshing and Vibrant

Maybe your pool is a kiddie pool in your backyard, just right for your feet. Maybe it's your neighbor's backyard above-ground pool. Maybe it's just your own bathtub, filled with cool water on a hot day. Mixing up one of these special cocktails will keep you right where you are if that's what you love. Or you can close your eyes, take a sip, and transform that kiddie pool into a turquoise plunge, overlooking the warm ocean waters. Fresh towel, anyone?

PALERMO VILLA PARTY

*A gin cocktail is the perfect drink to have in hand during a chic—
and wild—party night. The astringent bite of the gin, lime, and
Aperol are balanced by the smoothness of rosé wine. Mix this up
and serve it with a chunk of lime in a frosty wine glass, preferably
under the stars, surrounded by gorgeous people—or just your own
gorgeous self.*

1½ ounces gin

1½ ounces rosé wine

½ ounce Aperol liqueur

½ ounce fresh lime juice

Add the gin, rosé, Aperol, and lime juice to a cocktail shaker. Add
ice and shake for 30 seconds until chilled. Strain into a wine glass
over fresh ice.

SPARKLING ENTERTAINMENT

*Dripping with emerald vines and brilliant scarlet and orange
tropical flowers—you, of course—and your sparkler of a
cocktail. Now's the time for white linen, a bathing suit, flip-
flops, and lychee syrup combined into a delectable mixture of
sparkling wine and limoncello. Lemon balances the sweetness
and rosé turns this concoction a beautiful shade of pink. Pour
this into a glass over ice and take it out by the pool. Front
porches work beautifully as well—or your favorite chair pulled
up in front of the fan. Resort sipping can happen anywhere.*

1 ounce limoncello

½ ounce Lychee Syrup
(page 15)

½ ounce fresh lemon juice

3 ounces sparkling rosé wine

Lemon wedge or 3 peeled
and pitted lychees, for
garnish

Orchid blossom, for garnish
(optional)

Add the limoncello, Lychee Syrup, and lemon juice to a cocktail shaker.
Add ice and shake for 30 seconds until chilled. Strain into a wineglass
or spritz glass over fresh ice. Top with the sparkling rosé. Garnish with a
lemon wedge or three lychees, and orchid blossom (if using).

GINGER PINEAPPLE MOJITO

A traditional Cuban mojito is the perfect rum punch, usually made with rum, sugar, lime, and mint. To bump up the flavor to resort level, replace the sugar with homemade ginger syrup and add pineapple juice for more fruity sweetness. This spicy combination will cool you down even as the ginger turns the heat up a notch. Mix up two and clink glasses with your best poolside partner.

5 fresh mint leaves

½ ounce Ginger Syrup (page 15)

2 ounces white rum

1 ounce pineapple juice

½ ounce fresh lime juice

1 ounce soda water

Fresh mint sprig, for garnish

Add the mint leaves and Ginger Syrup to a highball glass and muddle gently. Add ice, the rum, pineapple juice, and lime juice. Stir with a bar spoon to combine. Top with the soda water. Garnish with a sprig of mint.

CLASSIC APEROL SPRITZ

The Aperol spritz is a very Italian cocktail, combining the bittersweet citrus liqueur with bubbly prosecco. As you mix it, watch the liquid turn a brilliant orange. Serve this spritz in an oversize goblet—using a stemmed glass keeps your fingers from warming the delicious libation inside. This is a drink you'll want to sip cold.

3 ounces prosecco

2 ounces Aperol liqueur

1 ounce soda water

Orange slice, for garnish

Add ice to a spritz glass or large wineglass. Add the prosecco and Aperol. Top with soda water and stir with a bar spoon to combine. Garnish with an orange slice.

MANGO AWAKENING

A tequila sunrise gets a Thai twist here, as we swap out the orange juice for a juice of a tropical kind—in this case, mango, which lends the drink a softer note. Grenadine adds a beautiful crimson blush to the bottom of the glass—perhaps reminding you of the sunrise over the Indian Ocean?

2 ounces blanco tequila

4 ounces mango juice

½ ounce grenadine

Cocktail cherries, for garnish

Fill a highball glass with ice. Add the tequila and mango juice. Slowly pour in the grenadine and let it sink to the bottom. Garnish with cocktail cherries.

FROZEN MANGO PIÑA COLADA

Is there anything that says "beach vacation" more than a piña colada? The fruity, creamy combination of coconut and lime is only enhanced by a healthy pour of rum. Here, we've added mango chunks for a tropical twist. Get out your blender for this one and top with a slice of fresh mango and a straw.

1½ ounces white rum

1 ounce pineapple juice

½ ounce cream of coconut

½ cup frozen mango chunks

Mango slices, for garnish

Wooden cocktail pick/ stirrer (optional)

Add the rum, pineapple juice, cream of coconut, and frozen mango chunks to a blender. Blend until smooth. Pour the frozen mixture into a hurricane or rocks glass. Garnish with mango slices.

TROPICAL RENEWAL

We've shaken up a resort-style libation with mango syrup, juice, and coconut water complementing the rum. Best enjoyed with the accompaniment of fresh white towels, lounge chairs, and sparkling pool water.

2 ounces white rum

1 ounce Mango Syrup
(page 16)

1 ounce fresh lime juice

1 ounce coconut water

Lime twist, for garnish

Fresh basil sprig,
for garnish

Add the rum, Mango Syrup, lime juice, and coconut water to a cocktail shaker. Add ice and shake for 30 seconds until chilled. Strain into a rocks glass over fresh ice. Garnish with a lime twist and a fresh basil sprig.

COCONUT DAIQUIRI

What's a pool lounge chair without a daiquiri? It's like sand without water—or you, with empty hands. Don't let that happen. Take control of your resort cocktail destiny with our Coconut Daiquiri. When the sweetness of the coconut syrup collides with the sharp tang of lime, all run through with rum, that combination just calls out, "You're on vacation!"

2 ounces white rum

¾ ounce purchased coconut syrup

1 ounce fresh lime juice

Lime wheel, for garnish

Add the rum, coconut syrup, and lime juice to a cocktail shaker. Add ice and shake for 30 seconds until chilled. Strain into a chilled hurricane glass. Garnish with lime wheel.

VESPA-TINI

The southern Italian liqueur limoncello gets our summertime engines going with vodka instead of gin (no opinions, please!). Splash in fresh-squeezed lemon juice and sweeten with a little simple syrup. Just try not to drink too many before climbing onto the back of that Vespa.

1½ ounces vodka

¾ ounce limoncello

½ ounce fresh lemon juice

½ ounce Simple Syrup (page 12)

Lemon ribbon, for garnish

Add the vodka, limoncello, lemon juice, and Simple Syrup to a cocktail shaker. Add ice and shake for 30 seconds until chilled. Strain into a chilled martini glass. Garnish with a lemon ribbon.

REBIRTH SPRITZ

*A wine spritzer is among the most perfect of summer drinks—
refreshing and cold with soda water balancing the alcohol. Here,
prosecco and lychee liqueur combine in homage to the famous
resorts of Italy and Southeast Asia. Serve this drink chilled in
an elegant champagne flute, drop in a lychee at the end, and
enjoy the bubble show.*

1 ounce lychee liqueur

3 ounces prosecco

1 ounce soda water

Lemon slice, for garnish

Lychees, peeled and
pitted, for garnish

Add ice to a large wineglass. Add the prosecco and lychee liqueur.
Top with the soda water and stir with a bar spoon to combine.
Garnish with a lemon slice and a lychee.

ISLAND INFUSIONS

Local Ingredients

You've been traveling for *quite* a while.
First a taxi, plane, then a boat—definitely
a boat because you're going to an island.
And look, you're here. Step onto the
dock. We've been waiting for you and
surprise! We've mixed up a few cocktails,
all created with an eye toward a special
island experience. Lemony, berry-y, nutty,
coconutty, mixed with delicious spirits and
plenty of ice. Take one. It's time to relax.

COCONUT MARTINI

Classic martini, dirty martini, dry martini—they're all delicious, whether they're shaken or stirred. But you're on vacation, aren't you? Or at least pretending to be? In that case, your life calls for something a bit sweeter, a bit more luxurious. Here, vodka takes the place of gin and cream of coconut combines with lime for the perfect smooth-tangy flavor pairing in a tropical take on the favorite drink.

2 ounces vodka

1 ounce cream of coconut

½ ounce fresh lime juice

Lime wheel, for garnish

Shredded coconut, toasted, for garnish

Add the vodka, cream of coconut, and lime juice to a cocktail shaker. Add ice and shake for 30 seconds until chilled. Strain into a chilled martini glass. Garnish with a lime wheel and shredded coconut.

HAWAIIAN OLD-FASHIONED

Sometimes, you just need something to sip when you're perched on the balcony of your suite overlooking the gold-flecked sea at sunset. Perhaps you're in the mood for an old-fashioned, that most traditional of cocktails, but with an island twist—here in the form of spiced rum, instead of bourbon, spiked with sweet coconut syrup. Select a glass, then strain this delectable mixture over rocks.

2 ounces spiced rum

½ ounce purchased coconut syrup

2-3 dashes Angostura bitters

Pineapple slice, for garnish

Cocktail cherry, for garnish

Add the spiced rum, coconut syrup, and Angostura bitters to a mixing glass. Add ice and stir with a bar spoon for 30 seconds to chill. Strain over 1 large ice cube in a rocks glass. Garnish with a pineapple slice and cocktail cherry.

FORTUNE–TELLER HIGHBALL

You've got a fortune teller ready to share secrets. You're cuddled on a luxurious velvet couch, ready to listen. But wait! First you need a drink—of course, you need a drink. Our highball replaces the traditional whiskey or scotch with amaro, that most Italian of liqueurs. A twist of lemon adds a note of sharpness— just enough to keep you on your toes in case those secrets are ones you're not quite ready to hear.

1½ ounces amaro

4 ounces ginger beer

Lemon twist, for garnish

Fresh mint sprig, for garnish

Fill a highball glass with ice. Pour in the amaro and then top with the ginger beer. Stir with a bar spoon to combine. Garnish with the lemon twist and mint sprig.

THE ITALIAN DREAM

Adding liqueurs to tequila vaults our European-style margarita right over the sun-washed cliffs of Sicily and onto the yellow beaches of the Mediterranean Sea. Amaretto lends warm nutty notes while an orange liqueur gives the cocktail a citrus punch, further enhanced by a squeeze of lime. This drink deserves a big goblet or a tumbler—also you, your favorite margarita-drinking partner, and ocean breezes.

1½ ounces blanco tequila

½ ounce amaretto

½ ounce orange liqueur

1 ounce fresh lime juice

Lime wheel, for garnish

Add the tequila, amaretto, orange liqueur, and lime juice to a cocktail shaker. Add ice and shake for 30 seconds until chilled. Strain into a goblet or tumbler over fresh ice. Garnish with a lime wheel.

MOUNT ETNA

Explosive? Not so much. Smoldering is how we like to describe this cocktail, with the delightfully bitter Campari warmed by a healthy pour of tequila. Grapefruit and lime add a kick of citrus, making this drink perfect for that person in your party who likes sharp over sweet—or who perhaps is sharp over sweet. You know who you are.

1½ ounces blanco tequila

¾ ounce Campari

1 ounce fresh grapefruit juice

½ ounce fresh lime juice

Lime ribbon, for garnish

Grapefruit slice, for garnish

Add the tequila, Campari, grapefruit juice, and lime juice to a cocktail shaker. Add ice and shake for 30 seconds until chilled. Strain into a rocks glass over fresh ice. Garnish with a lime ribbon and grapefruit slice.

SERENE SPIRIT MARGARITA

Spicy, sweet, and creamy—this is our Thai take on the margarita. Let the softness of the coconut milk temper the heat of the chile-spiced tequila—but not too much. After all, serene or not, we like this drink spicy—and you, too. Enjoy it strolling on the hot sand. We know deliciousness when we see it!

---

2 ounces Thai Chile-Infused Tequila (page 21)

1 ounce coconut milk

½ ounce fresh lime juice

½ ounce agave syrup

Lime wheel, for garnish

Add the tequila, coconut milk, lime juice, and agave syrup to a cocktail shaker. Add ice and shake for 30 seconds until chilled. Strain into a rocks glass over fresh ice. Garnish with a lime wheel.

BASIL OASIS

The gin and tonic is a peak-of-summer resort drink, perfect for sipping poolside. Ours is a green, vegetal version that muddles basil and cucumber slices with just a hint of simple syrup. Enjoy this fresh libation surrounded by tropical flowers and dripping vines—or perhaps in your own personal backyard paradise. It's going to taste delicious, regardless.

4 Thai basil leaves

3 cucumber slices, peeled

1½ ounces gin

1 ounce fresh lime juice

½ ounce Simple Syrup (page 12)

Thai basil sprig, for garnish

Add the Thai basil leaves and cucumber slices to a cocktail shaker. Gently muddle them to release the oils and juice. Add the gin, lime juice, and Simple Syrup. Add ice and shake for 30 seconds until chilled. Strain into a chilled rocks glass. Garnish with a Thai basil sprig.

SPIRITUAL RETREAT

*How is it possible to pack in so many serene notes in one drink?
We just tapped into the magic of a beautiful tropical spot, and it
worked. All the flavors come together in this vodka concoction,
including watermelon juice, which adds a unique flavor and
beautiful blush of pink. We recommend enjoying this cocktail after
a special spa treatment, surrounded by the flicker of candlelight.*

3 sweet basil leaves

½ ounce Lychee Syrup
(page 15)

2 ounces vodka

1½ ounces watermelon
juice

½ ounce fresh lime juice

Watermelon slice, for
garnish (optional)

Fresh basil sprig, for
garnish

Add the basil leaves and Lychee Syrup to a cocktail shaker. Gently
muddle the basil leaves. Add the vodka, watermelon juice, and
lime juice. Add ice and shake for 30 seconds until chilled. Strain into a
chilled martini glass. Garnish with a slice of watermelon (if using) and
a sprig of fresh basil.

ZEN ZEST GIMLET

It's hard to find a simpler cocktail than the gimlet: just gin, sugar, and lime. But we're not content with simple. We've elevated the classic cocktail here with a splash of green tea and another of ginger syrup—a bit of bitter, a bit of spice— all perfectly Zen.

2 ounces gin

1 ounce brewed green tea, cooled

½ ounce Ginger Syrup (page 15)

½ ounce fresh lime juice

Lime wheel, for garnish

Add the gin, green tea, Ginger Syrup, and lime juice to a cocktail shaker. Add ice and shake for 30 seconds until chilled. Strain into a chilled coupe glass. Garnish with a lime wheel.

MEDITATION MARGARITA

Ah, the bar. Just the place for liquid meditation. Slide onto a stool and raise a finger for the bartender. Order up the vacation drink we all crave, the margarita, but don't stop with a traditional one. Pouring a chile-infused tequila and adding three kinds of citrus flavors ups the decadence—and isn't that really what you need?

2 ounces Thai Chile–Infused Tequila (page 21)

1 ounce fresh lime juice

½ ounce orange liqueur

½ ounce Lemongrass Syrup (page 15)

Red Thai chile, for garnish

Lime wheel, for garnish

Add the Thai Chile–Infused Tequila, lime juice, orange liqueur, and Lemongrass Syrup to a cocktail shaker. Add ice and shake for 30 seconds until chilled. Strain into a rocks glass over fresh ice. Garnish with a Thai chile and lime wheel.

BOTANICAL BLISS

Floral Infusions

Colorful flowers add a special touch
to any drink, whether you're splashing
in elderflower liqueur or hibiscus tea.
We love botanicals in these cocktails—
after all, the islands are crowded with
blooms, both showy and delicate.
Steeping fresh or dried botanicals
infuses these creations with a luxury
resort touch that screams—or perhaps,
murmurs—serenity and bliss.

ITALIAN WELCOME COCKTAIL

Checking in? How delightful. Welcome. Perhaps you're hot and sweaty from your journey? Try one of these spritzers— it features elderflower liqueur for a floral note, refreshing grapefruit juice, and prosecco. You are in Italy, of course— or at least . . . you can imagine you are with this icy concoction in your hand.

1 ounce fresh grapefruit juice

½ ounce elderflower liqueur

3 ounces prosecco

1 ounce soda water

Grapefruit slice, for garnish

Fill a highball glass with ice. Pour in the grapefruit juice and elderflower liqueur, then top with the prosecco and soda water. Stir with a bar spoon to combine. Garnish with a fresh grapefruit slice.

HIBISCUS RUM PUNCH

Poured over plenty of ice and served in a beautiful glass, our Hibiscus Rum Punch pairs the floral note of the tropical bloom with the warmth of dark rum. Citrus juice adds a tart sweetness to this special libation. Brew hibiscus tea more or less strong depending on how much flavor you want and don't forget to enjoy the gorgeous orange hue as you mix and sip.

2 ounces dark rum

1 ounce brewed hibiscus tea, cooled

1 ounce pineapple juice

½ ounce fresh orange juice

½ ounce fresh lime juice

Pineapple wedge, for garnish

Orange peel, for garnish

Add the rum, hibiscus tea, pineapple juice, orange juice, and lime juice to a cocktail shaker. Add ice and shake for 30 seconds until chilled. Strain into a rocks glass over fresh ice. Garnish with a pineapple wedge and orange peel.

HIBISCUS SUITE

At the end of the day, when the sun is casting its long, warm, golden rays on the patio, shaking up a ruby-orange Hibiscus Suite will feel like the perfect closing note. White rum stays in the background here, while the fruitiness of the hibiscus tea contrasts with the bitterness of Aperol and lime. Sip this curled up on a silk sofa with a cashmere throw around your shoulders—or just imagine that you are.

2 ounces white rum

1 ounce brewed hibiscus tea, cooled

1 ounce fresh lime juice

½ ounce Aperol liqueur

½ ounce Simple Syrup (page 12)

Lime wheel, for garnish

Hibiscus petal, for garnish (optional)

Add the rum, hibiscus tea, lime juice, Aperol, and Simple Syrup to a cocktail shaker. Add ice and shake for 30 seconds until chilled. Strain into a chilled Champagne coupe. Garnish with a lime wheel and hibiscus petal.

SIAMMO TUTTI GAY

A Moscow Mule is a special summer drink served in a distinctive copper mug—you know the one. It's usually just vodka, ginger beer, and lime juice. But we're not about "just" at The White Lotus. Our mule is more than a little extra, with warming tequila replacing the vodka and delicately flavored elderflower liqueur offering a botanical flourish. But hang on to the copper mug for serving—the cold metal will help keep this delicious cocktail cold.

1½ ounces blanco tequila

½ ounce elderflower liqueur

½ ounce fresh lime juice

4 ounces ginger beer

Lime wheel, for garnish

Fresh mint sprig, for garnish

Cucumber flowers, for garnish (optional)

Add ice to a copper mug or highball glass. Add the tequila, elderflower liqueur, and lime juice. Top with ginger beer and stir with a bar spoon to combine. Garnish with a lime wheel, mint sprig, and cucumber flowers (if using).

LIFE OF THE PARTY

The bright orange Aperol is a quintessentially Italian liqueur brewed from bitter rhubarb, gentian root, and cinchona, a type of tree bark. Mixing it with elderflower and simple syrup tempers the medicinal bite that some people love, others detest. Jiggle the ice in your glass after you shake up this cocktail and take a long sip. You might be thinking: Oh, hello there. Welcome to Italy. Let the party begin.

1½ ounces Aperol liqueur

1 ounce elderflower liqueur

1 ounce fresh lime juice

½ ounce Simple Syrup (page 12)

Lime slices, for garnish

Add the Aperol, elderflower liqueur, lime juice, and Simple Syrup to a cocktail shaker. Add ice and shake for 30 seconds until chilled. Strain into a rocks glass over fresh ice. Garnish with lime slices.

BUTTERFLY PEACH TEA

The butterfly pea flower is native to Southeast Asia. Infused in vodka, it turns the clear alcohol a beautiful purple color. Add homemade honey syrup and peach juice and the added acidity will further transform your cocktail into a brilliant lilac hue. Strain into an icy rocks glass for a very special, very violet, very tropical resort tea.

1½ ounces Butterfly Pea Flower–Infused Vodka (page 19)

1 ounce peach juice

1 ounce brewed black tea (cooled)

½ ounce Honey Syrup (page 12)

Lemon wheel or cucumber slices, for garnish

Blue pea flowers, for garnish (optional)

A dd the Butterfly Pea Flower–Infused Vodka, peach juice, cooled black tea, and Honey Syrup to a cocktail shaker. Add ice and shake for 30 seconds until chilled. Strain into a rocks glass filled with ice. Garnish with a lemon wheel or cucumber slices.

JASMINE SOUL REVIVAL

Imagine that you've just arrived on the island. Doesn't that jasmine smell incredible? Our island is just dripping with it. Here, try our special cocktail made with our own jasmine syrup from those same beautiful flowers. We've mixed the syrup with gin and lime juice for a cocktail that boasts a marvelous floral bouquet. Have another sip. Welcome to paradise.

2 ounces gin

1 ounce fresh lime juice

¾ ounce Jasmine Syrup*
(page 16)

Lime twist, for garnish

Jasmine flower, for garnish
(optional)*

Add the gin, lime juice, and Jasmine Syrup to a cocktail shaker. Add ice and shake for 30 seconds until chilled. Strain into a rocks glass over fresh ice. Garnish with a lime twist.

*If jasmine flowers are hard to find, look for jasmine syrup from an online source.

PARADISE FLOWER

Could there be a better combination of flavors than the dark warmth of crème de cassis blended with the brightness of pineapple and lime juices? We've shaken up this fruit-filled libation just for vacation days when the sun is bright, and the lounge chairs are waiting with clean and fluffy beach towels for that post-swim refresher.

2 ounces light rum

1 ounce pineapple juice

½ ounce crème de cassis

½ ounce fresh lime juice

Pineapple slice, for garnish

Pineapple fronds, for garnish

Add the rum, pineapple juice, crème de cassis, and lime juice to a cocktail shaker. Add ice and shake for 30 seconds until chilled. Strain into a rocks glass over fresh ice. Garnish with a pineapple slice and pineapple fronds.

LYCHEE HARMONY MARTINI

For our resort martini, we've kidnapped the staid cocktail from the clubroom and whisked it away to the resort paradise of which we've all been dreaming. Using both fruit and syrup from a can of tropical lychees and a very special swirl of floral jasmine syrup, the martini gets a welcome tropical twist—and you get a sweet, frothy cocktail to carry with you from the pool to the beach and back again.

2 ounces vodka

1 ounce lychee juice
(from a can of lychees)

½ ounce dry vermouth

½ ounce Jasmine Syrup*
(page 16)

3 peeled and pitted lychees

Add the vodka, lychee juice, dry vermouth, and Jasmine Syrup to a cocktail shaker. Add ice and shake for 30 seconds until chilled. Strain into a chilled martini glass. Garnish with three lychees on a bar pick.

*If jasmine flowers are hard to find, look for jasmine syrup from an online source.

CALMING CHAMOMILE SOUR

With the addition of soothing chamomile tea, we've added a botanical edge to our take on a gin sour. The tea-time theme continues with homemade honey syrup instead of simple syrup. Shake, strain, and add a whipped egg white for an appealing foamy texture. Feel free to skip the egg white if it doesn't speak to you—but don't skip this drink. Otherwise, what will you sip at the lounge bar?

2 ounces gin

1 ounce brewed chamomile tea, cooled

¾ ounce fresh lemon juice

½ ounce Honey Syrup (page 12)

1 egg white*

Miniature orchid petals, for garnish

Add the gin, chamomile tea, lemon juice, Honey Syrup, and egg white to a cocktail shaker. Shake vigorously without ice for 30 seconds. Add ice and shake again for 30 seconds until chilled. Double strain into a chilled coupe glass. Garnish with miniature orchid petals.

*If you have food safety concerns, you may wish to avoid drinks with raw egg whites.

MOCKTAIL ESCAPES

Non-Alcoholic

Sometimes you want a special drink without spirits—something for the morning, something for the morning after, or something for that night when your liver needs a bit of a rest. In that case, we're here for you with recipe after recipe for escape-worthy mocktails that won't make you look longingly at your neighbor's G&T. You've got your own libation right here, with the teas and juices that make for the perfect liquor-free refreshment.

TRADEWINDS SUITE

Piña coladas are decadent resort libations, where the creaminess of coconut marries with tangy pineapple and fresh lime. But occasionally, you might want a mocktail version—perhaps even a cerulean mocktail version? You and your drink will perfectly match the cloudless sky, the foaming waves—and even the decor of the luxurious Tradewinds Suite.

1 ounce coconut water

½ ounce non-alcoholic blue curaçao syrup

1 ounce pineapple juice

½ ounce fresh lime juice

1 ounce soda water

Lime slice, for garnish

Orchid blossom, for garnish

Add the coconut water, non-alcoholic blue curaçao syrup, pineapple juice, and lime juice to a cocktail shaker. Add ice and shake for 30 seconds until chilled. Strain into a hurricane glass over fresh ice. Top with soda water. Garnish with a lime slice.

VACATION MORNING RUN

When you're done exercising, whether that means an invigorating run on the beach or a slow stroll from your breakfast table over to your poolside chair—you choose—mix up one of these fizzy refreshers to take with you on your cool-down. The grenadine at the bottom of the glass will give a lovely sunrise effect, making this the perfect start-your-resort-day drink.

4 ounces fresh orange juice

1 ounce grenadine

1 ounce soda water

Orange slice, for garnish

Maraschino cherries, for garnish

A dd the orange juice to a highball glass filled with ice. Pour in the grenadine and let it sink to the bottom. Top with soda water. Garnish with an orange slice and maraschino cherries.

OCEANSIDE MOCKTAIL

*Minty and fruity, with a tang from two kinds of fruit juices,
this is the drink to make when you want something a little
luxe to sip on the beach—or on a lawn chaise in the backyard.
Muddling the mint leaves extracts their oils and brings out their
fresh flavor, while the soda water adds a welcome jolt of fizz.
Shake and strain for a chilled, island-worthy treat.*

4 fresh mint leaves

½ ounce Simple Syrup
(page 12)

4 ounces pineapple juice

1 ounce fresh lime juice

1 ounce soda water

Mint sprig, for garnish

Pineapple wedge,
for garnish

Add the mint leaves and Simple Syrup to a cocktail shaker and
gently muddle. Add the pineapple juice and lime juice. Add ice
and shake for 30 seconds until chilled. Strain into a highball glass
over fresh ice. Top with soda water. Garnish with a sprig of mint and
pineapple wedge.

THE WHITE LOTUS
SPA COCKTAIL

Need a little me time? Think white bathrobe, thick towels, soothing music, and a delicious drink to sip. This hydrating concoction mixes the vegetal notes of cucumber with the richness of coconut water, brightened by the freshness of garden mint. Take your glass with you into the treatment room. Or just enjoy it on your front porch, perhaps with a fan blowing on you—your own personal spa.

4 fresh mint leaves, plus more for garnish

¼ cucumber, peeled and sliced

½ ounce Simple Syrup (page 12)

3 ounces coconut water

Cucumber ribbon or slice, for garnish

Add the mint leaves, cucumber slices, and Simple Syrup to a cocktail shaker and gently muddle. Add the coconut water. Add ice and shake for 30 seconds until chilled. Strain into a rocks glass over fresh ice. Garnish with a cucumber ribbon or slice and a few mint leaves.

SOUL RECHARGE

When your soul is feeling a little empty, try filling it up with this unique partnership of coconut milk and homemade Thai chile syrup. This special mocktail combines rich creaminess with a powerful spicy kick—and all without alcohol. Fresh mint and a splash of lime add freshness and balance. Keep extra Thai chile syrup in your fridge to add to martinis, gin and tonics, or any drink that could use a hint of tropical heat.

5 fresh mint leaves

2 ounces coconut milk

1 ounce fresh lime juice

½ ounce Thai Chile Syrup (page 17)

Lime wheel, for garnish

Add the mint leaves to a rocks glass. Gently muddle the mint to release the oils. Fill the glass with ice. Pour in the coconut milk, lime juice, and Thai Chile Syrup. Stir with a bar spoon to combine. Garnish with a lime wheel.

WELLNESS SANCTUARY

When you feel the need to retreat to an inner sanctum, take a minute first and mix up one of these luxe concoctions, with hydrating coconut water and refreshing watermelon juice. Shake together with lime juice and a bit of simple syrup, strain over ice, and take your glass with you into your own private retreat. You'll feel better in no time.

2 ounces coconut water

1 ounce watermelon juice

1 ounce fresh lime juice

½ ounce Simple Syrup
(page 12)

Watermelon slice,
for garnish

Fresh mint sprig,
for garnish

Add the coconut water, watermelon juice, lime juice, and Simple Syrup to a cocktail shaker. Add ice and shake for 30 seconds until chilled. Strain into a rocks glass over fresh ice. Garnish with a watermelon slice and mint sprig.

NAMASTE OR "NAMA-STAY"

Sometimes, you need a little break from spirits. But not a break from interesting. With our ginger, lemongrass, and fresh mint blend-up, interesting will be the first word you say after you take a sip. Once it's mixed up in a tall glass, this elegant brew is a gorgeous golden color, too. Namaste to you.

4 fresh mint leaves

¾ ounce Lemongrass Syrup (page 15).

4 ounces brewed ginger tea, cooled

1 ounce fresh lemon juice

Fresh mint sprigs, for garnish

Add the mint leaves and Lemongrass Syrup to a cocktail shaker and muddle gently. Add the ginger tea and lemon juice. Add ice and shake for 30 seconds until chilled. Strain into a rocks glass over fresh ice. Garnish with mint sprigs.

ENERGY HEALING FIZZ

You're feeling a bit depleted. You need an energy boost. And this is the perfect mocktail—spicy ginger beer doctored up with tart pomegranate juice and tangy lemonade. It's the perfect tasty sip to recharge your batteries and set you up for what's sure to be a fun evening ahead.

1 ounce pomegranate juice

1 ounce lemonade

4 ounces ginger beer

Lemon peel, for garnish

Pomegranate seeds, for garnish

Fill a highball glass with ice. Add the pomegranate juice and lemonade. Top with ginger beer and stir with a bar spoon to combine. Garnish with a lemon peel and pomegranate seeds.

VITALIT-TEA

Let's say it's the morning after an extra-fun night. You need a little health boost, perhaps a small liver cleanse. This earthy-sweet sip is the perfect addition to your breakfast. Green tea offers antioxidant benefits, with pineapple and lime juices, providing just enough tartness to wake you up. Add a chunk of pineapple and some mint to the glass—oh, and don't forget to make one for your partying partner. They need a bit of a boost, too.

3-4 fresh mint leaves

½ ounce Honey Syrup (page 12)

2 ounces pineapple juice

1 ounce brewed green tea, cooled

1 ounce fresh lime juice

Pineapple wedge, for garnish

Fresh mint sprig, for garnish

Add the mint leaves and Honey Syrup to a cocktail shaker and muddle gently. Add the pineapple juice, green tea, and lime juice. Add ice and shake for 30 seconds until chilled. Strain into a rocks glass over fresh ice. Garnish with a pineapple wedge and a mint sprig.

ZEN BREEZE

Sip on this combination of tropical fruit juices and coconut milk and you'll picture yourself on the balcony of your luxe suite, feet splashing in your personal plunge pool as the sun rises behind the palm trees. Try it—and block out reality, just for a few Zen morning minutes.

2 ounces mango juice

1 ounce pineapple juice

1 ounce coconut milk

Mango or pineapple slice, for garnish

Add the mango juice, pineapple juice, and coconut milk to a cocktail shaker. Add ice and shake for 30 seconds until chilled. Strain into a highball glass over fresh ice. Garnish with a slice of fresh mango or pineapple.

INDEX

ABOUT THE AUTHORS

RECIPES

SARAH GUALTIERI is a Long Island–based recipe developer and photographer. She works with beverage brands to develop cocktails and mocktails for the home bartender. Sarah's passion for mixology stems from her love of exploring different ingredients and their potential to elevate the drinking experience. Beyond mixology, she shares her culinary adventures on social media, inspiring others to try new recipes and techniques in their own kitchens.

TEXT

EMMA CARLSON BERNE is an author who often writes about food, history, and pop culture. Her other books include *The Ultimate Driving Book*, as well as the thrillers *Never Let You Go* and *Still Waters*. Emma lives in Cincinnati. More on Emma can be found at emmacarlsonberne.com

INSIGHT
E D I T I O N S

Insight Editions
P.O. Box 3088
San Rafael, CA 94912
InsightEditions.com

CEO Raoul Goff
VP Publisher, Weldon Owen Roger Shaw
Publishing Director Katie Killebrew
Executive Editor Edward Ash-Milby
VP Creative Chrissy Kwasnik
Art Director and Designer Megan Sinead Bingham
Production Designer Jean Hwang
VP Manufacturing Alix Nicholaeff
Sr Production Manager Joshua Smith
Sr Production Manager, Subsidiary Rights Lina s Palma-Temena

Weldon Owen would also like to thank Jennifer Newens.

Photography Waterbury Publications, Inc.
Food Stylist Jennifer Peterson

ISBN: 979-8-88674-210-7

Manufactured in China by Insight Editions
10 9 8 7 6 5 4 3 2 1

ROOTS of PEACE   **REPLANTED PAPER**
Insight Editions, in association with Roots of Peace, will plant two trees
for each tree used in the manufacturing of this book. Roots of Peace
is an internationally renowned humanitarian organization dedicated to
eradicating land mines worldwide and converting war-torn lands into
productive farms and wildlife habitats. Roots of Peace will plant two
million fruit and nut trees in Afghanistan and provide farmers there with
the skills and support necessary for sustainable land use.